T0147457

The Rope

Unravel What Is Choking You

Mary Ellen Hawkins Staffeld

WESTBOW
PRESS
A DIVISION OF THOMAS NELSON

WestBow Press books may be ordered through booksellers or by contacting:

WestBow Press
A Division of Thomas Nelson
1663 Liberty Drive
Bloomington, IN 47403
www.westbowpress.com
1-(866) 928-1240

Because of the dynamic nature of the Internet, any web addresses or links contained in this book may have changed since publication and may no longer be valid. The views expressed in this work are solely those of the author and do not necessarily reflect the views of the publisher, and the publisher hereby disclaims any responsibility for them.

Any people depicted in stock imagery provided by Thinkstock are models, and such images are being used for illustrative purposes only.

Certain stock imagery © Thinkstock.

ISBN: 978-1-4497-4285-0 (e)
ISBN: 978-1-4497-4286-7 (sc)

Library of Congress Control Number: 2012904348

Printed in the United States of America

WestBow Press rev. date:4/23/2012

Contents

"Unravel What Is Choking You"

Don't choose to remain in the boat bound by ropes not going anywhere. I challenge you to cut this rope, the one that has for a lifetime, entangled your true destination.

Pain comes in different circumstances and forms of life. Each and every one of us has experienced some form of pain or you might be a specific individual who at all cost avoids uncomfortable circumstances.

If you are that type of individual, trust me it will eventually catch up with you. Is this why you are looking for some kind of relief at this moment? Have you ever looked up the definition of the word "rope" as I will give you the very picture God gave me in comparison of my life and maybe yours. I am sure each and every one of us has seen the huge ropes on a ship that holds it in place. ***Take a good look at them and realize the weather, wear and tear, pulling and tugging that these huge ropes have endured and are so tightly woven you could never try unraveling them. Ever tried pulling one apart? It will automatically try and curl back together not wanting to separate. Sound familiar to your past or emotions? After reading this book you will know how to cut you rope.***

"Unravel What Is Choking You"

God's Revelation of the Word Rope

1) Rope: A thick strong cord made of fiber twisted together, (the last of this definition is interesting), "to catch with or lasso, know the ropes," to be well acquainted with a procedure; to entice or trick into doing something. Sound familiar?

2) Noose: A loop in a rope formed by a slipknot compared to Satan and his schemes so the loop tightens as the rope pulls, eventually cutting off airflow. Is this you? When oxygen does not get to our brain we do not think wisely. If not corrected we will eventually die.

3) 3) Lifeline: A rope or line for saving a life, as one thrown to a person in the water. Remember the show, "Who wants to be a millionaire"? They could call a lifeline partner to give them the answer. We may be the two above described but there will always be a way out through Jesus Christ our Lord and lifeline.

DEDICATION

This book is dedicated to God the Father, Son and Holy Spirit as He guided my hand to write most of this book over a period of six years.

To my mother, who is gone to be with the Lord, as she always loved me unconditionally and encouraged me to be all that I could be no matter what my circumstances.

My three children, Anna, PJ and Jack, who survived my quite adventurous yet often catastrophic life. I also was a victim of the "The Rope."

Grandchildren, who loves their "Nonnie" when at times it seemed as no one else did; Mazzey Ellen, Mason, Payton, Briley, and of course the adventurous 5 yr old twins, Noah and Landon.

My brothers, Blake, Mike and Dudley, as they taught me to be tough!

To my step-sister Vivian who is always there for me.

♫A little note to all my Irish kinfolk: May you always have a song in your heart and a smile on your face and a one and only cousin/niece from Texas that truly inherited some Irish lifestyles! My cousin Terri whom I admire for being one of the strongest Irish women, who if anyone knows what trials and tribulations are, she does and by the Grace of God keeps on ticking.

All across the country the co-workers I have encountered. May God Bless You and Keep You Safe. Yes, I know what you all are saying; "the one that always stirred the pot" has resurfaced. Just a little humor but probably true.

Last but not least, to all the people I have hurt in life. Words cannot express how sorry I am, as I too was a victim of not cutting my rope.

THE ROPE
CHAPTER I

PART I

THE SELF- SUFFICIENT SIN

All over the media and in entertainment, we cannot escape talk about different kinds of addictions. Conversations revolve around alcohol, drugs, sex, fornication, and adultery, but let's talk about a very lethal addiction called *"self-sufficiency."* I bet some of us have never thought about that addiction! Self-sufficiency is reliance on ourselves. We have become so stagnated with ourselves, thinking that we deserve the credit for who we are and the position that we hold.

Ask yourself, being truly honest, the questions below:

What would you do this very second if...

1) Your wife/husband, or girlfriend/boyfriend, called while you are reading this book and said he/she did not love you anymore and they have been seeing someone else. Maybe they just left you a note. Perhaps you saw them with someone else. How many times have we snooped only to find out something that delivers a devastating blow?

2) Your boss just called and said you no longer have a job. To make matters worse, you have a family to feed and maybe elderly parents to take care of.

3) The hospital called and the love of your life is about to die—your children, grandchildren, parents, brothers, sisters, husbands, wives, whomever it may be. That one phone call totally causes you to become comatose.

4) You get in your car to go to the store and on the way home you pull over for a fire truck to pass. You turn the corner and staring you in the face is the fire truck now in front of your home. Now you are looking at what took you thirty years to pay off, and it is literally gone up in smoke. Nothing, absolutely nothing, is left.

Even worse, your family had just spoken with you from that very home. You stand unable to breathe because of the shock.

Trust me, I have been there several times and no, I am not saying my hurt was worse than yours. I know, "by the grace of God" not all of us have been through what others have.

Maybe you are reading this book because something has knocked you off your feet. You may be grasping at everything in sight to help the pain. Eventually, you'll find out, it's only temporary relief.

Yes, you worked hard to climb the ladder, but guess who gave you the stamina to get there.

Did you ever think about the One who created you and will give you *only enough* oxygen to do what He created you to do? No, not what you desire for yourself. Think about it for a minute while I repeat this again: Do you trust the One who created you? This is where it all starts, so listen up!

Do you know the definition of "create?" It means "to cause to come into being." Examples of human creation linger in history. How well did the passengers on the *Titanic* trust the engineers that built the ship? They entrusted their lives on this ship. Further back in history the public laughed at Noah as God instructed him on how to build the Ark.

Look at the whole picture of how we really, honestly trust everyone and everything to make us happy—except God, our Creator.

How stupid are we not to believe in our Creator with our lives, the One who is perfect and perfectly creates?

He actually built us from the ground up. He knows every hair on our head (yes, it says so in the Bible in Matthew 10:30) and every thought that we capture. How, in His name, can we not believe in a master builder that is beyond belief if you stop and consider the complexities of our bodies? For one thing, in our flesh, we cannot comprehend if we don't see it in front of us.

There is nothing on this earth that can compare to the human body. Look at all of our body parts and think about it. Our brain actually tells our entire body what to do. They have tried for years and still have not been able to make a robot that could add up to our human bodies. If they did, which would never happen anyway, do you honestly think the thing would be running after the seventy or ninety years that some of us live?

I challenge you to really consider your body. Take a look in a mirror, or command your toe to move, wave your hand, get up and walk.

Do you get the picture? Quite a miracle, don't you think, if you ever examine it? We as fleshly humans do have a brain. Although we fail to use it while we are temporarily blinded by an unknown force (Satan, an expert in this field of blinding) or when it comes down to entrusting or relying on everything but Jesus Christ. Is the noose so tight around your life that it cut off the airflow to your brain?

When we are living for the One who created us who does not always guard you from that devastating phone call, He will be your own personal mechanic to put your parts back together. How much would it cost to have a mechanic or carpenter follow you around twenty-four hours a day/365 days a year in case your car broke down or something broke at your house?

Those are only material things. Think about how much it would cost you to have a psychologist follow you around 24/7 and diagnose your every thought and prescribe medication to try and fix you.

They would all have a heart attack following me around. Yes, I know I probably have a few detached wires that seem to short out quite often.

Sometimes it is not always traumatic reasons we change seasons. Sometimes the roping process occurs when we are enticed to leave our comfort zone and for some unknown reason it turns into a nightmare and we are left to deal with it.

As I was writing in the middle of the night in Austin, Texas, a water cooler suddenly drew my attention. An audible voice—whom I know to be God—stated: "Do you see that cooler?" I am like, "Yeah, and are you going to drown me or something?" He stated, "Why do you think that cooler would sell more than an ordinary cooler?"

Then I saw the word "industrialized" stamped on the cooler. As I felt goose bumps popping up all over me, I answered in my head, "Because it has been through this process to make it stronger."

He, in his infinite power, immediately began to show me a building supply company that mostly sold finished products. I listened as He spoke intensely to me—trust me, He had my undivided attention—as he said, "When I am through molding you, I will put you on the shelf, and you will be industrialized and ready to sell!" What a promise!

On another occasion, I had left my family for a time and finally returned to my family. The devil had me blinded for quite some time before he actually scooped me up. As a matter of fact, it took a year and six months. As I returned home, I was hanging on to every thread of God's promises to stay in the place I was at and try to live a normal life. But it wasn't easy. I felt uncomfortable in church, going back to the community from where I grew up after such a long separation. Then one day I was home alone with my children one night as they were asleep.

I heard an urgent voice (God once again), for me to go to the chapel that our church had owned. It was open 24/7 and smelled like an old catholic church. I can recall I fought for a couple of hours testing this voice because of leaving my children as my husband was at work. So I ventured out and decided that I felt it was God so my children would be in his hands. I arrived and walked in and turned the light on, scared to death I might add.

Nothing happened at first, so I am like "hello anyone home, it's me, wasn't that you telling me to come down here in the middle of the night!" All of a sudden, my hair blew over my shoulders as a wind had come through the chapel. We had no fan or air in this building as I felt this breeze. So I am really scared now, he is going to crucify me right there in the middle of town! I cried uncontrollably as I was devastated by what he told me. He stated in a very loud audible voice that he was going to take my son away from me and that is all that was said. I was devastated as I begged for forgiveness and to take my life and not my son.

I cried lying at the altar, until I fell asleep. I could not believe what I heard nor could I move or much less breathe. God had spoken to me before my son was born. He in an audible voice spoke to me while sweeping my kitchen floor telling me that I was to have a son. So now I am really confused at the fact that He, himself, gave me the child only to take him away. He awakened me out of my stupor and said these very words: ***"That is how much I love you. I gave my only son for you and your sins."***
I left there and went back home and did not sleep for days as I could not comprehend how much he loved me.
I want you all to know that is the truth. He did give his only son for us. His Son was a very humble man that never even tried to get back at anyone. Nor even defend his sinless self after being brutally beaten and spit on and crucified on a cross. How petty are we to think how bad we have it. How busy are we not to stop to help someone or even give them a phone call. If that's the case we are too busy and maybe we need to remember Gods great commission in life is that **"all"** to know about Him.
No matter the color, shape or size that is our commission. I challenge you to pick up the phone or go visit someone that needs you and maybe prayed for you at one time.
Just remember He will only give you that air that you just breathe for His supply, not yours, as we become callous to His purpose of our being. Our oxygen tank has HIS numbers on it and when it is over there is nothing we can do to replenish it. Not by ventilators, medications or any other life prolonged facilitators. Live today with a purpose that He gave us as we never know when our time is up.
I have had a catastrophic life to say the least. Constantly with no avail, trying to unravel my rope and never cutting it off completely. Always in denial of the person I was, the family I destroyed and who I was meant to be.

THE ROPE
CHAPTER I

PART II

REPAIR OR REPLACE THE ROTTEN DECAY

As an Insurance Adjuster, another phase of my life, God again showed me the parable of a home structure and a dentist. Yes God, in his infinite parables of life can reveal anything to you as long as you are where he wants you to be.

As a dentist he sees rotten decay as a severe pain that can be fixed. He knows how long this tooth has decayed and knows the surrounding areas need fixing first, which would be antibiotics.

Heal the area and then work on what happened in the beginning get the picture? This process in which we all know is an exposed nerve, so filling it up will do no good until the pain is so unbearable an entire root canal is done removing the pain. It never gets this way overnight nor will the dentist fix it when you walk in. It must be healed and then replaced. As an insurance adjuster you have the words stuck in your head: "Remove and Replace."

You must remove the bruised structure to replace the remaining structure to hold the firm foundation.

Not only in a storm but normal routine maintenance on a home. If you don't replace rotten decaying lumber it will eventually cause problems to the entire structure. You cannot continually "patch and replace" and expect everlasting future.

I could name probably a 1,000 items off the top of my head if you don't maintain it will be of no use. The cost you in the long run, will be ten times more than if you would have replaced one rotten decaying piece of the structure. Again, I am sure you are asking yourself what all this has to do with me and why I am reading this book.

Stop and compare your life right now with what the Holy Spirit just concluded.

I bet you could define that one rotten piece of lumber in your household (as comparison to your life) that could have been fixed a long time ago. However, you or the responsible person in your family were too busy to stop and fix it and now the whole structure is falling because of the one and only board you chose to not maintain is rotten and cannot be fixed. How about your vehicle? There is maintenance on everything in life that is not eternal. Have you ever thought about that? Not just material things, your marriage, your relationship with your family, etc., I could go on and on. Life and family is way more important than a checkup at your local oil changing station, tire rotation or whatever you think is important. So stop now and take a check on when the last time you put new oil into your family, or rotated the tires so one does not feel they have more expectations on them than any other part of the family.

Let's talk about planting, there can also be decay and rotting if the plant does not come up fast enough. Seeds are planted in the ground but as they grow they emerge above the soil after watering they begin to break ground to indulge in feeling the sun. Even from the beginning God has constantly drawn a picture even before mankind, trees, and plants, were reaching for the light.

Most of us have planted gardens or seeds and if they don't spring up fast enough they will rot in the ground never amounting to anything. The day they emerge out of the ground to reach the sun they have to be nurtured as with anything else. This would be watering, fertilizing and pruned every day to become the plant that would reproduce and multiply for more seeds.

Life is an everyday miracle growing process, no end, just everyday reaching for the "Son." We will never get to a resting place because we would shrivel up and die or rot in the ground as we have a purpose in life and need to grow each day.

THE ROPE
CHAPTER I

PART III

WHAT FREEDOM REALLY IS

Based on our beliefs throughout history it is a common understanding that we basically live our lives as always said, "America the Free." We were taught by society that we have the freedom of speech and are protected by our rights. I agree to a certain point that we do need to be protected when it comes to certain laws, although the definition of freedom does not coincide with the freedom that God wants us to have.

I have said before, He is the creator of our body and soul, He knows what makes us tick. Have you ever seen a child that has not been disciplined? I personally do not like being in the presence of one and neither does anyone else.

The only one that cannot see this is the parents. The child runs around, butting into the conversations and totally needing to have the whole entire room to be their audience. Parents somehow have the perspective that they don't want to hurt their feelings, because they love them so much. Children now days are allowed around the parents and adult gatherings, often times interrupting conversations, with adults. To my astonishment, the parents will look at the child to answer them and leave you forgetting what you were saying. Number one the child is left to believe they will always have the floor without any respect to their elders! They only have to speak up and butt in, not only in this area, but are allowed their opinion anytime and anywhere. In my experience with working with CPS (Children's Protective Services) and in my own surroundings, I have known these children to grow up and be total wreck. Mainly because of the freedom they were allowed and the outcome is catastrophic. **Reason being, there have never been any limitations, therefore there are no expectations.** What may have seemed at the time they loved them, now the children disrespect them and in return the child is now in **bondage**.

The parents have actually allowed the child to be head of household. Make sense? Well if not, just let your little one do anything they want today. Also take note of your surroundings when you have company. Do you hear yourself whispering around your children? Do you constantly tell them to go play? Think about it, I know we all have at one time or another, but done over and over you will have bad results, as this sends messages to your children.

In turn they realize that there are **no limitations because you have set no expectations.**

In other words there are no limits to what we are allowed to do in life as this causes a never ending feeling of "if it feels good, do it syndrome."

This is the biggest trap of all creation. As we live this lifestyle in freedom we begin to be in bondage, or a noose, of a never ending slavery of our own self or involuntary manslaughter is a better word for it. Reason being we will be on a never ending search for happiness because we were never disciplined as children and allowed to go anywhere and speak when we felt like it.

Therefore we did not have to listen at home so why should anyone else tell us what to do.

The whole point I am trying to reach is the same scenario with Jesus Christ our Father. We as undisciplined fleshly beings and honestly think that we can do anything we like. Can you not remember a time when you fit that child's description of getting away with everything as an adult. Trust me, ask my brothers we did not get away with anything unless we were sneaking and God forbid our parents found out. Well so I will say there should definitely be a balance of discipline and trust with children. If not they will wind up as I did trying to live my childhood as an adult and was very catastrophic. I thought, as this message is all about, that I was free to do as I wanted. Being I was in bondage as a child with my earthly father I swore once I got out from under his what "he thought was discipline," more like a Concentration Camp to me, I would say. I won't go any further on this subject as there will be another book. The reason he did the things he did, as it does trickle down through life to the next generation and childhood wounds from his life.

I am sure we have all experienced hearing people in life state how free they are from a spouse, job etc. to do as they please. Well from my experience, that old freedom runs out real quick only to discover that you are in **bondage of seeking just one more adventure, boyfriend, husband, trip etc.** You are now in unwanted slavery. You have no limitations because you as an adult, have expectations of what was supposed to be fun and end up in Romeo and Juliet, stock market gamble, that "just one more time syndrome," although you lost everything. A million other expectations, adultery; you just knew he would leave her, or she would leave him and now you are the one left at the curb and their lives continue. Let's talk about **expectations** a minute. Why do we expect people to understand our life and to deal with us when they don't have a clue. Reason being, they have not lived our life like and we have not lived theirs. This would be also in the bible; "as you have done it to the least of mine you also have done to me." Meaning that the poor, the alcoholics, the drug addict, "the least," of these. You gave them drink when they were thirsty, fed them when they were hungry and clothed them when they were naked. We might want to stop and think when the last time we did any of those things to a complete stranger. No, not your neighbor or your Christian friends, God says the "least."

We have all heard the following, Jesus was not at the Country Club when he met the woman at the well trust me. Not driven to the last supper in a Limo either. Get the picture or should I say BOX? This is my point if you are unequally yoked with a mate or friend trust me they will think you are thrown off. Some even think I live for the drama, as I have been told oftentimes. Have you ever felt like "Dear Abby" the newspaper columnist that tried to answers everyone's problems? Hello! That would be me. Now let's talk about what I mentioned above "The Box". The reasons some people cannot discern where people like us are coming from is become some choose to live in the box they have been in their entire life. It is not our place to judge anyone. They could not go through life not helping people if they had the Holy Spirit living within them. Trust me after receiving the Holy Spirit I thought I could save the world. Although, I am only human and fell by the wayside several times to say the least. My "lifeline" caught up with me for the rest of the chapters in my life.

Like in the beginning of this book some of you choose not to reach out to others as we are called, to avoid pain and suffering. Everything in your world is just fine in your little "box" and that is ok in your eyes.

Have you ever wondered why a "box cutter" has not virtually ripped the side of your box open into your life? If this did happen and you taped it up to avoid becoming involved, guess what. You just cut off your airflow of getting a blessing. You might have thought, "Wow, I missed that little nip!" However, what about the person outside the box who did not even have a box for a shelter?

Yeah, you did real good you stayed all safe and sound in your own little box, however God saw you ignore that person and hunch down hoping they would go away.

Well next time you might not be so lucky. Maybe the person that needed you accidentally one day picked you up and threw you out to the curb. You felt a kick and was thrown against your box tumbling down the street! The next thing you hear is a big noise of a garbage truck! "Oh my oh my, if I would have just stuck my head out!" If I

would have not been so selfish maybe they would not have thought I was just garbage and threw me to the curve. Now my life is being crushed beyond recognition.

I am lying helpless with all this garbage as I have been thrown into this rotten, smelly pit and no one knew I was inside my box. I was hiding in my box so I did not have to deal with their problems. Now I need them, oh if I would have just opened a little hole of faith outside my box. God showed me this box and people's lives that absolutely do not get out of there "little box" because they feel their little world is just fine without anyone interrupting there schedule. We are all busy in life, but again if it's just a mere "hello," it might just be the word someone needs to hear and they were noticed. We live in a world of disconnected I would call it. We now, text instead of hearing a voice. I actually see couples and families eating out and all of them on the phone texting someone. Also this particular new wave of texting has proven to cause more divorces and breakups as you can sit next to your significant other while texting your boyfriend, girlfriend, etc. This will be another book as I will leave this alone for now. Always trying to get more, do more, and be more in half the time.

In the end we will leave all this behind as it states also in the bible the chapter in Mathew 6:19-21. It merely tells us not to lay up treasures that will rot and thieves will break through and steal, but lay up for yourselves treasures in heaven for where your treasure is, there will your heart be also. My mother was the angel in my life. I never understood until I began to grow older but she would always say these very words: "follow your heart." **Freedom is being able to discern what or where that freedom will lead you.** Will you really be free in the end of the choice you make? I lived in another country that the government totally ran. It was terrible how the citizens bowed down to rules and regulations but seemed to except it because they grew up in that environment and never knew any different.

We do live in a country that we have the rights and freedom, although people choose not to get involved because they are in **bondage of their own little world**. So I ask you again about God's "great commission." We all need a self- check sometimes. I will admit we can become immune to life as well as anything else just going through life doing what you are supposed to do. Not really caring just making a paycheck.

Trust me it can be one family out of fifty that may change but that one family counts. Jesus states, as you will read in another chapter, he will leave his herd to find the single one that is lost. You are free in this country to find that single sheep that needs encouragement.

He or she has only a single thread of hope and that may be you or maybe God is leading you to read this book because you are the wondering sheep. At this time you are wondering is there anyone out there that really cares about one single person out of billions.

You may be someone that just lost everything and it's sad to say but now you have no friends because you can't entertain them anymore with all that you had. So now you realize maybe they were not your true friends. Just the other day in church a pastor stated: "Sometimes God has burned all your bridges and you can only go forward with him." I truly believe as in this book you cannot unravel your rope at times, you must choose to cut it completely, starting over.

Climbing to the top will cause you sometimes to slide down the rope and hopefully there will be a knot in "the lifeline" (Jesus Christ) to catch you. Sometimes He will allow you to fall to realize that you only need Him to pick yourself up in this trying time. God has been with me time after time and has never let me down. He chose me to be the hand to give us all these chapters that lie before us.

I did not deserve this by any means, but will tell you no matter where you have been or what you have done it is never too late with Him! As a matter of fact you will be the very one He will use because you have been through the fire and can honestly help others.

THE NOOSE
CHAPTER II

PART I

ENTICEMENT OF PEEPING AROUND THE SHIELD

DO YOU REALLY WANT TO PLAY THE GAME?
This chapter will enlighten you on playing around with sin while God continues to be our "shield." The definition will tell you in its own words, as it has several different meanings: 1) A broad piece of amour carried on the arm or in the hand 2) A person or a thing that guards, protects or defends 3) something shaped like a shield to protect or conceal with or as if with a shield.

Psalm 144:2 we all know; My Goodness and my fortress, my high tower, my Deliverer, **my shield**, and in whom I trust, who subdue my people under me.

When you are behind a shield nothing can hit you, harm you or touch you. If you step to the side, on either side, or in front of "shield" you are in the target area of getting hit. Then does it not make sense to stay behind the "shield" out of harm's way? Easy to say, but not after years of venturing out continuously as it becomes a habit.

We have a tendency to want to constantly "peep" out from behind the shield. An explanation of peep is to look through a **small opening** or from a concealed location 2) come partially into view 3) a quick "furtive look" in which furtive means: taken, done, or used by stealth, sly, shifty. So as we would say often "sneak a peep."

What we don't realize at the moment a small opening can cause **death**, that's all it takes often times! Look out for a short quick moment and **BAM,** you are dead! To me worst case scenario I myself have encountered my entire life it seems like would be this example: You keep peeping out over long periods of time constantly wanting to see more and more so guess what? You are now learning how to **"dodge the bullets"** and growing quite experienced at it, so you think.

As your flesh begins to thicken, your mind is anchoring in on "dodging the bullets" and certainly does not have time for discernment.

You grow accustom to this lifestyle thinking that you dodged the bullet. God will only allow you to dodge so many before he lets you get hit! We never know how big it will be or how small and painful as sometimes the small things in life wind up being a thorn in the flesh that never goes away! Yes, I have experienced this and it is horrible.

Bullets or ammo, whatever you would like to call it, I learned about them at gun shows and people in my life that hunt. There are some that are made to go all the way through their target without exploding and there are also "hollow points" that explode on impact.

One day you just might peep out around that shield just one more time and a so called "hollow point" might be coming your way. So ask yourself "can I take just one last look?" You be the one to decide if it is time to quit sneaking a peep. After all who knows you might have quite a few shots left however, you might lose everything in a blink of an eye.

We have all heard our children say **"just one more time momma,"** have you not? Gets pretty irritating as they know our weakness, and we let them do it just so that will be the end! Really? I don't think so that just leads to another "just one more and I promise!" I won't say which brother but oh my you know who you.

Every time my mother would send us to our room I would go in and do something to occupy myself. Gee not him!

He hollered the whole entire time we were confined to our room.

I can still hear him saying: Please momma, I will wash the dishes, clean the house, just let me out crying and banging on the door. Think that's funny, he even would get down and holler through the air conditioning vent. Now do you not think God gets pretty fed up with our "just one more time" as we are adults now? Trust me I know he wanted to put me down a many a time as I thought I was so experienced and again to say "I knew the ropes."

Yes, sorry and very apologetic to say the least, as I have experienced the just one more time scenario of peeping out from behind the shield. To say the very least, I should have gotten a Purple Heart!!

THE NOOSE
CHAPTER II

PART II

IMPULSE TURNS TO REPULSE

IMPULSIVE HABITS BECOME A LIFETIME OF MISERY.
Well we all could identify with this term I am sure. I used to think it was pretty neat to be so unpredictable, living on a whim or whatever you would prefer to call it. I still am somewhat impulsive until one day the word "impulse," got me to thinking about the word "repulse." Impulse is a particular inclination that leads to an action.
Ever feel like just driving off into the sunset and just wind up wherever? Yes, I have done many things on impulse and I will say some were great and some were horrific!!
Have you ever been in a state of mind that would fill a garbage dumpster? In that moment we would do anything to get out of that awful feeling of our surroundings.
Probably anything would look good and sound great. Not always eternal do we make good choices that are only a temporary fix.
Our eyes want to look at something pretty and will always at the time, make you feel good. Once we are in a position of being in that pretty little ambiance then we need to take it a step further.
Take something simple as getting in a new car. You went to the dealership and really just wanted to see what was new on the market, however the brain reacts to the eyes and therefore just looking is not enough. So we decide to take the ambiance a little further and step inside to sit behind the wheel. Trust me there is nothing that smells better than a new car. Funny, how when the payments come due the smell wears off.

It's kind of like everything else in life when the new wears off and we toss it aside and go onto something else. Trust me, I thought long ago when I was a child and did not even know about the "flesh," I often wondered why we were spending money on the moon when a lot of people were so poor. I know there are reasons for everything when it comes to technology but at the time I did not understand.

Later in life I began to realize how the flesh will never be satisfied and that is how the world turns. Look at where we are today compared to only ten years ago. I do believe we could be living on Mars if we kept going. This is some of my point: There is always someone out there that is going make something better than what is on the market right now. Some of the time, it is the very person who created the object and just keeps on taking it a step further. Therefore, by the time it's out for a few months its obsolete. So guess wha? You can't even buy parts for the old one now so you must buy the new one. The flesh will never ever stop, not saying this is always bad in the market sector but let's look at something else.

Going back to impulse and seeing how harmful this could be, let's think about that high we got when we stepped into that new car. It was great at the time but after the new wore off, not to good now that you are living beyond your means.

Now I am going to get to the nitty gritty. There are reasons for seasons as I have always said. God allows fun impulses in our lives to see what happens when it all turns so repulsive and we are left standing by the dumpster and would give anything to get rid of that horrible sinful feeling. The feeling we had in the beginning as we were in the dumpster feeling lonely, depressed, broke, etc. so we took it upon ourselves to reach out for some impulse.

Go ahead let's do anything today that comes our way to make us feel good!!! We have been there and trust me the consequences that lead our impulse are way worse than that feeling you had in the beginning. Again, the flesh will never reach that ultimate high you once felt. For some the first time you smoked marijuana, that one last fling when you cheated, the first drink you had and danced all night, because as these things continue, they as everything else grow old and you are on something new.

Until you hit that dead end road to repulse and everything becomes disgusting to you because there is no fun and you spend your last dime trying to get that feeling again with no results then God can restore you. When this happens there is a never ending road to amazement and what God will surprise you with next.

After living on impulse for all of your life I will admit it is quite hard to live a normal life. The thought of living an 8-5 life is tremendously scary to say the least.

Maybe that is why I have had so many occupations in the past. Also, other things out of the norm because habits are habits and like anything else they are very hard to break.

I, when living as I did, would hear people say they have been at their jobs 15, 20, 30 years and I just could not comprehend. These people went to the same place every day and lived in the same house for so many years. My mother also, trust me, she was my anchor of all anchors! I often think of all the places I lived and trust me it all started after I graduated. I think I moved to 7 different places the first year. Ask my brother as he would not answer the phone after a couple of times moving me. I still today don't know where I will be in a year!

I actually prayed to God to let me be a missionary I was so tired of moving at one time I thought OK I have had enough practice surely He is ready for me to go overseas!! Gosh forbid, because I am about to run out of places in the United States. Then often times I hear people say a rolling stone will gather no moss.

Well who ever thought that up? I never knew of a time that our Lord had a home even the same place for two or three nights in row. Here's another good one "don't count your eggs before they hatch!" The bible teaches us to speak as if it were! I know I am getting off track.

As our flesh continues to be impulsive and we are constantly looking for something exciting to come along. Habit forming it is, but when you have God in your life he will lead you each step of the way and you can fight the impulse. God will give you peace anywhere you are in life.

I will never forget the most awesome days I had when I lived in New Mexico. In the middle of no man's land (trust me)! God began to show me how to slow down and enjoy the simple things of life. All that were free, and of Him. Just with my eyes I saw the most beautiful hummingbirds all different colors, rainbows so close you could drive through them and you would turn gold. At the time there was snow on the ground as it covered the land (along with junk cars etc.) it what a peaceful sight. It was like a blanket covering all the noise you could hear a pen drop.

As I went into the mountains I never experienced anything quite as beautiful as the Aspen and Birch trees blowing in the wind and the sound they made. It was a breath of fresh air in my life as I was so used to running around chasing my own rainbows and then learned all I had to do is just **sit still**.

It's very hard to just sit still in life when you are the type person to make things happen. Everyone that knows me would tell you just that. I don't care how I did it, wrong, right, (improvised mostly) by the Grace of God, I would figure something out. I never understood why it would take so many people and so many hours to do something. I figure just do it and if it's wrong then fix it just at least make progress.

That also sometimes can be put into the impulse category in a good way I hope. Different strokes for different folks. I knew a particular person in my life that would study on buying something for years. They would actually read article after article on a particular thing before they made a move.

I will admit I have slowed down a bit but not quite that much. I am not saying that is a bad thing actually it probably is a good thing. Like I said earlier, by the time they purchase something they are sure to have the newest on the market as things rapidly change with technology.

All of this is to say be careful in life as habits become your lifestyle and impulse can turn to repulse if not recognized and dealt with.

THE NOOSE
CHAPTER II

PART III

EXPENSE OF EXPOSURE

Exposure has quite a few meanings as everyone knows. Mostly, meaning to uncover the bare facts that are sensitive and sometimes devastating. There is a difference in the spiritual world.

God will not allow anything in your life that would purposely destroy you. He will allow things to be revealed, to teach you and help you get rid of whatever you are hiding. Not exactly hiding from Him, because he knows and sees everything you do. However, if we expect him to manage our lives, we must be honest with ourselves and allow our true inner being to be exposed and dealt with. This is a very painful process at times. In the long run there is a hell and I would rather deal with exposure now before I faced an everyday torment. Exposure could also be a devastating blow that involved a mental problem that was revealed. Oftentimes people have laughed or ridiculed others not knowing this is a devastating lifestyle. It is an everyday torment that other people just cannot comprehend. For one thing they do not realize it is a sickness and sometimes even with medication it does not help. Now days the situation is worse because we have psychiatrist and pain clinics willing to dole out anything you think you need. Then you go through life trying to cover up the way you really feel pretending to be someone you are not.

This torment that I speak about is horrible and no you cannot suck it up and pretend because it is a medical diagnosis. No matter the medication you are prescribed, eventually you are immune to it and then it's time to be a lab rat again.

I totally understand the world's physical health needs and that is catastrophic to be bed ridden, crippled and so on and so forth. It is also a terrible thing to have mental issues because you are on a constant roller coaster throughout life.

Without God no one could survive any medical problems or mental torture to see you through it.

Mental suffering in the beginning, becomes undetected by the person as they are a child and are acting like a normal child.

However when things begin to unravel in your life it causes a great effect sometimes leaving a child withdrawn and not knowing really what to do.

I was very withdrawn as a small child after being molested at the age of five by friends of my parents that we always spent time with.

The patterns become horrible puzzles that cannot fit together no matter how hard you try to get involved with society.

This is where the downfall begins. As stated in a previous chapter you will turn in the direction that someone will make you feel important.

A mother figure however, can try to make up for a daughters lack of attention but it will never fulfill what God made in the beginning. A "father" is supposed to portray his love and shelter the female being and also the masculine one as God made him to be. Women are made from a man's side for him to watch over us from the very beginning.

A child's memory is the most delicate thing in life as that is where all my problems evolved from and I have learned in my past with my own children.

I will just say a divorce is the most selfish act that was ever created when you have children.

Mental situations are very hard to admit and under the influence of a counselor you are liable to just make some story up to hide the real hurt. This awful hurt goes twisted into cords for another round of other things that is curled up in the noose. Satan will lie to you making you think you can deal with a mental problem while totally destroying your life and the one's you love. God put doctor's on earth to solve that problem as after years of torment and living a catastrophic life I finally realized I had a problem that is hereditary and can live a normal life only on medication. Until you have experienced this abnormal lifestyle you cannot realize the importance of seeking a doctor with the right diagnosis. It is then you can be the person God created you to be.

THE LIFELINE
CHAPTER III

PART I

GET UNDER THE UMBRELLA AND STAY THERE

I have two words God has given me a comparison of and I will explain as I am typing. The first is "umbrella" and I am sure you all know what that is. As the dictionary states, it is fabric cover mounted on a stick for protection from sun or rain.

The other word is "faith." Let's see how this word coincides with the word "umbrella." The dictionary states that faith is confidence or trust in a person, loyalty, or fidelity.

Now to the best of my knowledge, I have had to go through some pretty tough trials to build up my "*faith.*"

Notice when you begin to open the umbrella it gets bigger and bigger, protecting more and more. This is a good example of building your protection for your entire life. The more you expand your faith the more your umbrella (God) will protect you.

Faith comes by believing when you cannot see anything visibly, but trusting in the omnipotent.

Yes that is a pretty scary word meaning: "having unlimited authority or power" as in Jesus Christ. I admit I never believed how much God was in control of my life all along. Even sometimes the circumstances I was in was not of God he turned them around for the good.

In the bible it states if only you have the faith of a mustard seed you can move a mountain. Pretty powerful statement I would say. A mustard seed is a very tiny seed. Let's go back to the word "omnipotent" and having unlimited authority is the first part.

We must not ever limit God with our expectations and saying this, why would you want to anyway if you think about it.

Let me give you an example in the bible. How about when God parted the Red Sea?

Can you imagine running from an army arriving on the beach front, totally surrounded by an army on all sides?

Well this really happened when God's people left Egypt. They came to the Red Sea with no place to go as chariots and armies followed them.

God parted the entire sea and made a way for them to cross! The bible does not lie, it is God's book.

As they began to cross, they continued to be followed. God released the sea on the army after they approached dry ground and the enemies drowned. This is only one miracle as there are many miracles in the bible.

We, I know are only human and sometimes we cannot see beyond our nose! **Sometimes it is raining so hard outside of our umbrella we cannot comprehend the rainbow that is coming up next.**

Have you ever tried getting into your automobile with your umbrella up? Pretty aggravating to say the least, as I know I have ruined a few cramming them into my vehicle to keep from getting wet. Ever see the old clotheslines that looked like an umbrella with no covering? Trust me my umbrellas look pretty scary to the point I don't think you would want to ride in my back seat. As my children used to say "it will poke your eye out." **God has showed me you can't use his umbrella when you are under another umbrella (the vehicle) because there is only one God.**

The most fascinating thing about having faith is you never know how God is going to fix your problem.

He often times will do it in way that there is no other way it could have been fixed other than a miracle from Him!

This is how he builds faith in us because it leaves you speechless in trying to figure out how He did it. There is two parts to the word "omnipotent." I just covered "authority," now let's talk about the word "power."

Would it not be nice to have a body guard by your side that had the strength of the Incredible Hulk? I use this illustration as my son used to rip his clothes up playing the Incredible Hulk as a child.

Try going up to a huge skyscraper and hollering at the top of your voice until the whole building crashed right before your eyes. That would be pretty powerful I would say. This really did happen in the bible as it states "By faith the walls of Jericho fell down as they chanted." All in all God loves us so much that he wants to be our umbrella and that is all He asks of us.

Just simply have faith that he can and will take control of your life and all of its problems.

So I will ask you this question. Why would you want to hold on to all of your finances, relationships, worries upon worries, drugs, alcohol and anything else in your life that is out of control? All you need to do is keep your umbrella up.

This does not come overnight, sometimes it takes practice. Remember what I said about getting into the car with the umbrella? How many times do we keep trying to get under some "other umbrella?" Time after time we try cramming Him in a place that already has a different cover that is not matching up with the cover He has provided us.

Just like the clothesline. We will be left out in the rain because there is no covering left on the one we crammed in the car!

THE LIFELINE
CHAPTER III

PART II

NITRO INDUCED

God gave the ultimate second chance to us when he sent his son to die for us on the cross.

Let me explain this to you if you have never read the bible. In the Old Testament, God made a deal with Abraham, the father of many nations, for him to be head of the household and he will raise his family in accordance to God's word if he is circumcised according to God's word. The deal was that it would be a token of the covenant (the deal) between the two. Now to be circumcised is to "remove the foreskin of," in other words "remove the flesh," in which God gave example of us removing ourselves (the physical flesh literally, so he can do His work in us).

Now the uncircumcised man child whose flesh of his own foreskin is not circumcised, that soul shall be cut off from his people, he hath broken the covenant. The soul is the spiritual part of a human being.

This was God's plan in the beginning with man and his covenant with man's soul, to join them together.

However, man's sinful nature overcame the process of circumcision, therefore, God created His Son "born of a virgin," so He could have absolutely no strings attached to man's sinful nature. Totally unbound, by man's flesh.

His Son was crucified, died on the cross and then resurrected so His spirit could actually live inside of us. He was no longer alive as in human state. This is the only way we can be redeemed is for the Holy Spirit to live in us. Reason being, you have absolutely no conscious when it comes to sin and will do anything you like because there is nothing in you that will convict you that you are wrong.

There are so many people walking the face of the earth thinking that just because they help people and go to church that they are going to heaven. Wrong, because you actually have to be accountable to the Holy Spirit if a little small voice in you says "don't do it." Even with the Holy Spirit we still sin sometimes but must get back up and dust ourselves off and ask for forgiveness.

There is nothing in this world that can make you feel so convicted as the Holy Spirit.

I know myself it is an everyday check on me because yes, I am human also. Then there are times when you stray away and you cannot seem to regroup and get that pure Holy Spirit to come back to you. This caused many a day in my life to be dark and empty.

If you are going to a church that is not growing and you do not feel anything but just going through the motions of going to church you better leave and find another one.

I cannot tell you enough about **dead churches.**

They are the ruination of every family, divorce, drugs, porno, you name it. Reason being you have no gas in that station to fill you up and make it last so you can get through the day.

Some of us need help just getting through the next 30 minutes. In my life as within CPS I would tell my clients that were addicted to drugs, alcohol, whatever the problem might be, to take 30 minutes to an hour each day and look at the clock. Get a tablet and write the hour down and know that you made it one hour without the drug so you will try another hour and so on and so forth.

This is not as overwhelming as taking it day at a time. Trust me I have been there, not with drugs but with relationships, when I thought I would never make it through the day.

One thing God my Father has taught me is to think of this life only to be temporary, in which it is. That helps if you know then you can hang in there and know you are going to a better place when you leave here, that is if you are saved. Right now, ask yourself: If I was to die right now reading this book or walking out the door and killed in a car accident, would I go to heaven or hell? If you do not know the answer that means you are not saved and no you are not going to heaven.

Ever wonder how you got back up when kicked in the mouth? I will call it "Nitro," as I have a brother that transported his company's Top Alcohol Funny Car and also worked in the pit. This is what kicks in when the car is to travel at top speeds. I must add they did win the 1995 World Championship NHRA!

Now there is also the "Holy Spirit." This is a breath of fresh air induced into our body when we repent of our wrong doings and ask Jesus Christ to come into our hearts to give us that second wind.

There are so many suicides and self-induced addictions because people have nothing in their lives to help them get back up. They must turn to another way to reduce the pain. Just let me say that this is a temporary fix as we all know it only makes matters worse.

THE LIFELINE
CHAPTER III

PART III

THE UMBILICAL CORD

For all of the father's reading this book, please take time to reflect your life with your daughter's. The effects of a father's love can enhance a lifetime of devastated lifestyles for your daughter. Reason being, you were her role model, being the only example of a man in her life during her childhood.

To me heartache caused by someone you love can be the most painful feeling in the body. The trust that you built up in this person all of the years or months, or should I say, "tried" to build up, whatever the situation. Only to be torn away from you on a daily basis. I have been in situations that left me speechless, unable to move, or at times unable to love again or even breathe. Starting as far back as I can remember my father ingested into me day after day as I was growing up, ridicule, hatred and the most painful was rejection. I would try my best to do everything my brothers did only to be constantly ignored. There was so much abuse that no one will ever know the heartache and torment that my mother and I suffered as my father suffered a horrible childhood unknown to me as I was growing up.

No one but a daughter can know the importance in a father's life as my lifestyle did continue on into my adulthood. Constantly seeking attention, only acquiring it from my mother, who always tried to fill a void with no avail. At a very tender age I could have never imagined what a catastrophic life I would lead.

This pattern was a repetitious cycle because it all started with 18 years of trying to gain recognition of the only man in my life, my dad.

Then there is **anger associated with rejection**. The word rejection has several words that describe it but one stuck out in my head and that is to **"discard"** and is **"useless or unsatisfactory."** That is how my father made me feel every day of my life.

Once anger set in it was an everyday feeling that I learned to deal with. However, not knowing that this trait would follow me throughout life it continued undetected.

The only reaction I had was to run from the deepest wound that had formed in me as a child. After many years of wasted relationships I realized how many people

I had hurt. Trying to escape that original incision that had torn my world apart on a daily basis, not knowing what love was or even giving it the smallest chance. I became so calloused that I felt no remorse as unconsciously I learned to protect that wound above all circumstances.

I suffered a very bad broken heart many a time. One of many was very devastating as I recall. You know if you have been through one of these, the "I can't breathe or even get out of bed, much less look at the world and pick myself up off the floor." Once again, I turned to my lifeline (Jesus Christ) to give me the strength to get through it and eventually he does. Have you ever had a particular song you constantly listened to during the hurt? I will always go back to that song just so I know how God did pull me through it!

I will not elaborate on this too much as I am sure one day maybe God will give me the courage to tell my story only to help others to know that they can outlive that incision.

You choose your mate as you grow up with a father figure, (like my dad) and that is the only man you knew. So statistics state that it is most likely the type person you will be attracted to.

Well we all have a profile we look for and trust me you could not have a tougher profile than my dad. He was one of kind! They definitely broke the mold when God made him.

So basically I would associate my profile of what a man was to be, watching my father.

So needless to say you were a wimp if you did not match up to him. I watched my dad's ways and the way he dressed.

My dad was a cowboy, a welder and had his own construction company. There was not anything my dad could not do! Whatever the job he would get it done. My dad also could dance and he was the best of entertaining, never meeting a stranger.

He had several boats and loved to entertain as I was growing up. Of course it was one of a kind and with plenty of engine pulling up to 9 or 10 skiers at a time. He had several motorcycles throughout his life.

My Father custom built his trucks with dual wheels, he always had something no else had.

Something happened to my Father when he was at a very young age that made him have a hatred

for women. So I won't go any further as he like me, carried this throughout his adulthood.

He had a lot of anger within him and yes it did not take much to make him outraged. I often felt sorry for my dad as he was a hard worker and seemed to struggle as he had such talent but had a wasted life as I traveled the same road.

He was constantly seeking excitement or something new, although my mother loved him very much she grew weary.

It's really sad to say but I never really knew my father. I finally forgave him on Father's Day of 2011 as I left the church early and went to his grave and wept. I knew then I had really forgiven him as I felt totally different from the times before. I began to get closer to my heavenly Father. Growing older I learned that I could have another Father (Jesus Christ) that would never leave me nor forsake me.

This somehow would seem to ease the pain as I cried out many a night for Him to just take me.

I see each day people living in misery and yes, I

have also been in this scenario not knowing what to do. My youngest brother always would say "when you don't know what to do don't do anything at all."

Well that doesn't set in very good with me as God did instill in me this very ambitious trait. Sooner or later I am back on the same path of destruction. God will continue to let satan lead you down these paths of destruction until you learn. I think I have finally got it not to depend on anything or anyone but my heavenly Father (Jesus Christ) to make me happy.

God has showed me that he has to rebuild me in His way not mine and His time not mine! I have for some time now been on medication also as I have stated in an earlier chapter. Time is a very strong essence when being rebuilt. How long is always the question? How long will I be in this pain? Well in the bible it states very clearly that whatever you sow in life you are going to reap it.

Let's start with the word "sow." This word means to scatter seed for growth. Often times we scatter bad seeds when we don't realize whether good or bad is what we will reap one day or another.

The word "reap" means to get as a return, recompense, or result. So basically whatever you do, it will one day return to you good or bad. Trust me it happens for the less fortunate because of wounds that were not taken care of, I have reaped many a year of bad seeds.

Sometimes individuals that come into your life are used as a tool for Satan. Beware of wolves in sheep's clothing. Sad to say but if you realize each time you go back to bad sowing you are only prolonging your reaping time.

I have learned this to be so true as in my life it was wasted like my dad's. God's timing is immeasurable. On day in your life might be a hundred in God's timing.

We tend to live in the flesh and worry about everything in sight. When all along what can we accomplish? That is the hardest lesson to learn. Give it to God and let Him take control. Focus on the words "it's not your life so stop doing what you are doing."

Temporary means "lasting or serving for a time only," not permanent. If we would focus on this word "temporary," life is too short to be angry at the world and your surroundings. I will admit sometimes it is a very hard thing to do especially when your childhood was messed up and your whole life turns into a temporary world. As in relationships, a permanent residence, "hello," are you with me anyone who has led a vagabond life? Just as you think "ok this is the one." I have made up my mind, thick or thin I am going to hang in there.

Well then the old incision is split wide open once again because there was no Godly foundation. As a matter of fact I probably was standing on sinking sand the time of that decision! So now I am at the starting line once again, running to pursue something to heal that incision that hurts so bad I can't even breathe. One morning at a church service the preacher had a sermon on the love of Jesus Christ.

As I was sitting there a light came on in my head (if there is anything to look at up there). Suddenly, I realized that absolutely no one can buy this love. No one can work hard enough to earn this love.

No one can receive enough points to get this love. People say "anything can be bought for a price." Not Jesus, because he paid the price that is free for us with his blood.

There is nothing that can make you feel the way He does. Absolutely nothing in the whole entire world can replace Him. Just think about it for a few seconds. People try to create everything in life to make them happy. As I often too, was always looking for that person, new car, job, shopping for a fix, anything to make me happy just for the moment. As we all know that feeling does and never will meet our expectations that we put on happiness. Should we not look to our Creator that put us together? Take this moment to seek Him out and feel that real happiness that only "He" (Jesus Christ) can give you. Rest assured it will be with you for a lifetime, with only one incision, that is deep within you and that is his Holy Spirit.

THE LIFELINE
CHAPTER IV

PART IV

FINDINGS OF THE ROPE

We will learn the process of learning how to unravel your rope. Let us now come to some conclusions after defining what would lead us to some revelations in our own lifestyles.

Below are some comparisons with life and the words such as:

1) root

2) core

3) foundation

This will help you to simplify all that you have read and hopefully unravel your rope or cut it completely off. You have a whole new life that begins and ends with Jesus Christ that will be your **"lifeline."**

Let's start with the word **"root."** Everyone knows what that is but this word has a very powerful meaning when comparing it to a human life.

Realistically, if we would take the time to get to the root of all the characteristics that make up a human being maybe then we would not be so quick to judge.

Maybe we would not be so quick to ignore a stranger or send a child on their way to the next grade for the next teacher to deal with.

Even more so working with CPS I have witnessed that genetics play an important part of abuse. If not dealt with this pattern becomes a way of life. Not only to the people involved but the environment goes unrecognized as it has just become the way they think life is supposed to be. Yes I have talked about this in previous chapters.

You and only you sometimes, are the one person in that family's life that can make a difference. Often times the problem can go on for generation after generation until something catastrophic happens and fingers are pointed but not fixed. Point the finger to yourself also.

Did you honestly do all you could do? Did you just do your job and get your paycheck? I often wonder how do we go unchecked day after day, month after month and year after year? God says he will leave the whole entire herd of sheep to save the one and only that has strayed.

A child is an innocent lamb. Have you ever studied a lamb? They are very co-dependent like a child needing a parent. They cannot be left alone without a shepherd as they can face many dangers and sometimes death. Think about this, it takes the learning process 365 days a year 24/7 and yes I am talking since the day you were born. The learning patterns from babbling to talking and walking. Like the old saying goes you did not get here overnight so the problem will not get resolved overnight.

You must go back and understand how you learn one thing by repeating it over and over until you accomplish it. One of my granddaughters used to state she was an expert when asked how she did something.

What I am trying to explain is that a pattern develops from the time you are born until you die. Your surroundings play an extreme role in your life. The word "root" as a plant, grows deep into the ground where it receives its nourishment and moisture to keep it living. As humans we grow up and are rooted by our family, friends and our environment and that is where we will get our nourishment. ***Sometimes sadly to say, it is not always nourishment it is survival.***

This will take us to the next word which is **"core."** This is the most essential part of a fruit that contains the seeds. This is where we will look at the example of, "everything in life has a beginning." The core started with a seed. So if you want to see the growth of an apple you start by peeling the skin, (outer surface that the world sees) then the inside is cut away to reveal the **"core"** and the seeds. (*outer surface that the world sees*) then the inside is cut away to reveal the **"core"** and the seeds.

This was the initial part of the apple's development. So the world sees a beautiful red apple that was picked for market. However the purchaser has no idea where the apple actually was planted and what the seeds went through to get picked.

Compare this to your life, go back and research how you got to where you are today. What all did you endure to make it to the market and why? Look at the very **"core"** of your life. Did you have a bad seed in the family? Let me relate to you that seeds are often distributed in other packages although they came from the same batch but were separated. I am trying to simply say that sometimes we don't understand were we came from or why we act the way we do.

Trust me this is sometimes a very painful ordeal but in order to unravel your rope or cut it off you must go back to the core of your seed. Just remember your lifeline (Jesus Christ) will be beside you every step of the way as this must be revealed to stop the choking process in your life.

Our next revelation will be the word **"foundation."** I have explained this word, in a sense, previously in the chapter, "Rotten Decay." Now that you have unearthed or revealed your bad seeds you will begin to realize what you need to unravel or cut off to start the new foundation.

This new "foundation" will be based on what you have learned in the chapter regarding "repair or replace." This word will give you and the ones around you, that you influence a sense of a more firm foundation that will endure existence.

So now you have unraveled your ancestry and you have just proclaimed that you will begin a **"new foundation"** with all new material. That would also include, **"the rope,"** that would not uncurl after numerous times you pulled it apart because you have chosen to cut it completely off.

Also, you are now aware of your environment and the lifestyles that created a **"noose"** around your neck. Therefore dust your pants off and rise again. I am not saying life is a breeze, but you now you have a **"lifeline."** Maybe you just needed some reassuring that your lifeline (Jesus Christ) came to rescue you!

Printed in the United States
By Bookmasters